Monkey Chinese Horoscope 2024

By
IChingHun FengShuisu

*Copyright © 2024 By IChingHun FengShuisu
All rights reserved*

Table of Contents

Introduce 5

Year of the MONKEY (Wood) | (1944) & (2004) 8
    Overview 8
    Career and Business 10
    Financial 11
    Family 12
    Love 13
    Health 14

Year of the MONKEY (Fire) | (1956) & (2016) 15
    Overview 15
    Career and Business 17
    Financial 18
    Family 20
    Love 20
    Health 21

Year of the MONKEY (Fire) | (1968) 23
    Overview 23
    Career and Business 24
    Financial 26
    Family 27
    Love 28
    Health 29

Year of the MONKEY (Earth) | (1980) 30
    Overview 30
    Career and Business 31
    Financial 33
    Family 34

    Love 35

    Health 36

Year of the MONKEY (Water) | (1992) 37

    Overview 37

    Career and Business 38

    Financial 40

    Family 41

    Love 42

    Health 43

Chinese Astrology Horoscope for Each Month 44

    Month 12 in the Rabbit Year (6 Jan 23 - 3 Feb 23) 44

    Month 1 in the Dragon Year (4 Feb 23 - 5 Mar 23) 46

    Month 2 in the Dragon Year (6 Mar 23 - 5 Apr 23) 48

    Month 3 in the Dragon Year (6 Apr 23 - 5 May 23) 50

    Month 4 in the Dragon Year (6 May 23 - 5 Jun 23) 53

    Month 5 in the Dragon Year (6 Jun 23 - 6 Jul 23) 55

    Month 6 in the Dragon Year (7 Jul 23 - 7 Aug 23) 58

    Month 7 in the Dragon Year (8 Aug 23 - 7 Sep 23) 60

    Month 8 in the Dragon Year (8 Sep 23 - 7 Oct 23) 62

    Month 9 in the Dragon Year (8 Oct 23 - 6 Nov 23) 65

    Month 10 in the Dragon Year (7 Nov 23 - 6 Dec 23) 67

    Month 11 in the Dragon Year (7 Dec 23 - 5 Jan 24) 70

Amulet for The Year of the Monkey 73

Introduce

The character of people born in the year of the MONKEY

People born this year have smart, cunning personality that is hidden behind cuteness. They talk because they are cute, they are fun-loving, they have intelligence that is easy to teach, and they can learn quickly. People born in this year are very attractive and charming. They are usually very interested in social gatherings. However, they rarely hide their own emotions because everything will come out on their faces as they get to know each other. People born in this year are excellent problem solvers. If you have a problem, they will always offer to assist you, will be a good listener, and will always suggest the appropriate words. Curiosity drives people born this year to constantly learn. The disadvantage of the Year of the Monkey is that there is sometimes a lack of reason. And you're ready to paint a picture for yourself and others to believe in everything people born in the Year of the Monkey do. Staying is always the best option. People born in the Year of the Monkey are perceived as selfish, opportunistic, and cunning by some. People born in this year are uninterested. Friends born in this year are devoted and loyal. Aside from that, you're a sweet-tempered but repulsive lover who fades quickly.

Strength:
You value unity and enjoy resolving problems for others.

Weaknesses:
You enjoy teasing others, and as a result, you are looked down upon; don't think twice before acting.

Love:
People born this year have a lot of love because they are cute, talkative, and talkative. In addition to extramarital affairs, they frequently manage their charms when they like someone and get to know each other without hesitation. People born this year as boyfriends look cute because they are calm, always consider the

feelings of others, don't like to fuss, frequently talk to each other for a reason, and if they still don't agree with someone, they will ask to be together for a long time. proof but if you find the person who likes you the most, just getting along with each other is enough.

Suitable Career:

People born in the Year of the Monkey are thought to be of the golden element. Architects, actors, artists, handicrafts, brokers, consultants, banks, and opening a shop selling construction materials are all professions that promote and suit your destiny. Working in metallurgy, machinery, selling automobiles or automobile accessories, iron ore, industrial plants, ceramics, selling jewelry, or even agricultural work Real estate development is a lucrative business for people born in the year of the Monkey.

Year of the MONKEY (Wood) | (1944) & (2004)

"The Monkey eats the fruit" is a person born in the year of the MONKEY at the age of 80 years (1944) and 20 years (2004)

Overview

This age cycle applies to the senior horoscope of the Year of the Monkey because the planet that circles into your horoscope this year is the Kok Ying star, which is a star that will result in advancement in your profession, including business. All of the abnormalities of the previous year will gradually go away. As a consequence, you will have little difficulty this year. There is only one thing you must remember: you must take care of your physical health. When traveling outside the home or over long distances, you should have your children follow and look after you for your safety. However, you will be more dejected and lonely this year than normal. Your children and relatives will be uninterested in you. What can assist with this is to let go and not cling to things that give you pain, whether they be the words or acts of others. Along with attending the temple and listening to sermons and the Dhamma, keep your mind tranquil and smile. Make your life all about happiness.

This is an opportune year for youngsters to study hard and have the bravery to show off their abilities in their field of competence. Gather experiences as life capital to be valued by instructors and parents, similar to how an embryo emerges from an eggshell and steps into the outside world. Which will expand its effect and have an impact on a variety of issues. The first is that your mood will change, causing you to get easily agitated. The obsession with temptations and numerous vices comes next. You will be easily swayed this year. Sometimes you lose control and end up going in the wrong way. What you should be wary of is the possibility of disaster and ramifications from driving and having an argument, or coming together to walk around and have a dispute with others, and be wary of quarrels and disagreements with others. Be wary of getting into trouble and becoming a criminal even if you did not commit the crime. You may have a criminal case and even be imprisoned.

Career and Business

This year, whether you're studying or starting a new job. Choose between studying at home and studying abroad. Everything comes down to your perseverance and commitment. Then you'll come across a customer who will assist you. Furthermore, the outcomes will be well worth the effort. Especially during the months when work and studies have good progress and prosperity, including the 2nd Chinese month (5 Mar. - 3 Apr.), the 3rd Chinese month (4 Apr. - 4 May)., the 7th Chinese month (7 Aug. - 6 Sep.) and 11th Chinese month (6 Dec. 2024 - 4 Jan. 2025) for entering into joint ventures and investing in various matters. You should be wary about your finances dwindling this year. Don't get taken in by flattery and investment solicitations. There is a good likelihood of discovering harm. Especially during the months that destinies in both age cycles should be especially careful of being deceived, namely the 1st Chinese month (4 Feb. - 4 Mar.), the 4th Chinese month (5 May - 4 June.), the 9th Chinese month (8 Oct. - 6 Nov.) and the 10th Chinese month (7 Nov. - 5 Dec.). Making any contracts, whether work or study, be extra careful. In the small details, be careful of being at a disadvantage.

Financial

This year's financial horoscope for both life cycles is favorable. Cash inflows come in two forms. purchasing Government Savings Bank lottery tickets, purchasing stocks or investing in stocks, conducting modest trades being a broker to help with trading, or collecting commissions from helping sell things or being hired to do extra labor will all provide you with a lot of unexpected cash. These items will assist you in putting money in your pocket. Especially during the months that support and encourage you to have good fortune, including the 2nd Chinese month (5 Mar. - 3 Apr.), the 3rd Chinese month (4 Apr. - 4 May), and the 7th Chinese month (7 Aug. - 6 Sep.) and the 11th Chinese month (6 Dec. 2024 - 4 Jan. 2025), but you should be careful during the month that your finances will be difficult. Both found fluctuations including the 1st Chinese month (4 Feb. - 4 Mar.), the 4th Chinese month

(5 May - 4 June), the 9th Chinese month (8 Oct. - 6 Nov.), and the 10th month of China (7 Nov. - 5 Dec.) prohibit others from lending money or signing any type of financial guarantee. Also, refrain from gambling and do not invest in illegal businesses.

Family

This year, the family is at peace and has received fortunate favor. The owner of fate has the criterion for purchasing pricey real estate. There is a good moment to move into a new home. There are guidelines for dealing with various fortunate occasions in the family, but you should be wary of those who encourage them. Don't listen to rumors from those who don't want to be negative. Especially during the months when there will be chaos within the family, namely the 1st Chinese month (4 Feb. - 4 Mar.), the 4th Chinese month (5 May - 4 Jun), the 9th Chinese month (8 Oct. - 6 Nov.) and the 10th Chinese month (7 Nov. - 5 Dec.) You should be cautious of mishaps that may occur among family members. Be wary of youngsters or servants who may cause problems, and be wary of things that may be damaged, lost, or stolen. You should also be wary of betrayal and slander from people who do not want you good.

Love

You must avoid becoming upset and interfering in your children's troubles for this year's senior fortune tellers. It will improve your family relationships with your children and grandkids, and they will respect you. You will be charming for your adolescent destiny. Someone of the opposing sex is extremely eager to get closer. The most important thing to remember is to not act too quickly. Don't be overly emotional and committed if you love someone. Because you are still young and have plenty of time to discover the proper partner, you should avoid the term disappointment. During the month that love will be a problem, quarrels, and chaos is the first Chinese month (4 Feb. - 4 Mar.), the 4th Chinese month (5 May – 4 Jun), the 9th Chinese month (8 Oct. – 6 Nov.), and the 10th Chinese month (7 Nov. – 5 Dec.) You must be careful of speaking with people of the opposite sex who can easily cause arguments. Beware of third parties interfering in the relationship. You should also not interfere with other people's family matters. When traveling to entertainment venues, be careful of contracting serious diseases. You should know how to protect yourself.

Health

Even this year, the seniors prefer to be alone with themselves. However, this is not the proper way to act. You should go out and make acquaintances your age and participate in things that you both enjoy, such as bird watching or Chinese boxing. Attend a merit-making or charitable event if you have the opportunity. You will be happy in later life, and you should let go of your children and grandkids. Consider that each individual has their unique worth. It would be preferable if you were present to advise and encourage them. However, there are some months in which the lords of both life cycles must pay special attention to their health, including the 1st Chinese month (4 Feb. - 4 Mar.), the 4th Chinese month (5 May. – 4 Jun), the 9th Chinese month (8 Oct. – 6 Nov.) and the 10th Chinese month (7 Nov. – 5 Dec.), increase attention to food hygiene. Be careful of seasonal infectious diseases. If any abnormalities are found, you should immediately see a doctor. Don't let the symptoms become so severe that they are difficult to cure.

Year of the MONKEY (Fire) | (1956) & (2016)

"The MONKEY in a herd" is a person born in the year of the MONKEY at the age of 68 years (1956) and 8 years (2016)

Overview

This year is regarded as an excellent year for the senior destined person of the Year of the Monkey, and fortunate fortune will come to you. Work, especially business, will be aided in its growth and prosperity. Money, fame, and status will all enter the picture, especially within the family, which will quickly find auspicious power of support, culminating in money and wealth filling the house. Furthermore, you will have the option to plan important events within your home this year, whether it is a birthday anniversary celebration, a wedding, a housewarming ceremony, launching a factory, building a new office, or having the opportunity to acquire costly property for the home. Bringing joy and smiles to the family. However, you must be cautious of the perils posed by the bad stars that will visit your horoscope this year, as you will unexpectedly face both the evil stars Go Xing and the stars Do Sua. This frequently has a negative impact, resulting in health issues. As a result, you must pay more attention to strengthening your immunity and being cautious of mishaps. Be wary of the risk of bleeding, as well as infections that might affect small children in the house. Seniors should be cautious of their moods this year, as they are easily agitated and irritable, and they prefer to be furious at others, producing issues for those near them. Throughout the year, be wary of quarrels and conflicts among members of the household, to the point that you may be unable to look at each other.

The fortunate star circling in the zodiac house for the child's future around this age is the Kok Ying star. As a result, your academics will progress this year. You should put in a lot of effort in your studies. Furthermore, parents should ensure that their children split their play and study time wisely. Review lessons, do homework, and turn it in on time as directed by the teacher. Then the gratifying outcomes will emerge. But there are more crucial things that parents should be aware of mischievous behavior from varied play or learning activities, falls and accidents, and notably hazards from water.

Career and Business

This year's work has patronage power, which aids in professional advancement. Another period of rapid growth is the expansion of the trade business. To develop new work, boost investment, or invest in new topics outside of previous concerns, it is required to identify an heir or helper to help continue the task. This year will see the appearance of outcomes that will provide delight. The months in which your work and business are prosperous include the 2nd Chinese month (5 Mar. - 3 Apr.), the 3rd Chinese month (4 Apr. - 4 May), the 7th Chinese month (7 Aug. - 6 Sep.) and the 11th Chinese month (6 Dec. 2024 - 4 Jan. 2025), but you should be careful during the following months that work will have obstacles, problems, and You should avoid various investments, including the 1st Chinese month (4 Feb. - 4 Mar.), the 4th Chinese month (5 May. - 4 Jun.), the 9th Chinese month (8 Oct. - 6 Nov.) and the 10th Chinese month (7 Nov. - 5 Dec.). Be wary of changes in the external economy that may have an impact on investment. You should also be wary of small accounting thefts, and you should be wary of signing contract paperwork that may cause complications in the future. Avoid progressive or rising penalties. A catastrophic loss can result if something goes wrong. As a result, before deciding to sign any contract, thoroughly weigh the advantages and downsides before signing.

Financial

This year's financial fortune is a very excellent income criterion, with cash inflows going in two directions. Both via regular income and supplementary revenue from other sources. As a consequence, when a good chance presents itself, you should utilize the money to advance your job, produce results, raise your income, and increase your investments to improve your income even more. During the months when finances flow smoothly and support you to have good fortune, they include the 2nd Chinese month (5 Mar. - 3 Apr.), the 3rd Chinese month (4 Apr. - 4 May)., the Chinese month (7 Aug. - 6 Sep.) and 11th Chinese month (6 Dec. 2024 - 4 Jan. 2025). However, it is good for outside investments in businesses that you do not know of. You harm the money in the system and may draw other funds into the entanglement, perhaps leading to a liquidity crisis. Therefore, you should analyze and consider environmental factors well before raising funds and avoid large investments during the following months: 1st Chinese month (4 Feb. - 4 Mar.), the 4th Chinese month (5 May – 4 Jun.), the 9th Chinese month (8 Oct. – 6 Nov.) and 10th Chinese month (7 Nov. – 5 Dec.)

Family

This year's family horoscope predicts that the family members will get favorable energy and money. There will be those who get jobs, pass tests, or win important honors. Honor, renown, and money will all be bestowed on you. You will also be able to purchase pricey assets. Have the conditions in place to conduct auspicious occasions in your home. But you should be careful during the month when there will be conflicts in the home as well as people in the house causing problems with people nearby, including the 1st Chinese month (4 Feb. - 4 Mar.), the 4th Chinese month (5 May. – 4 Jun.), the 9th Chinese month (8 Oct. – 6 Nov.) and 10th Chinese month (7 Nov. – 5 Dec.), As a result, you should not become engaged or intervene in the concerns of others. You should also be wary of people in the house bickering with neighbors, as this might ruin long-standing relationships. Keep an eye out for subordinates who misplace or steal things.

Love

This year's love horoscope for the senior fortuneteller is mild. You may experience some arguments or problems. Please be cool, check your remarks, and maintain good emotional control. Don't retaliate with violence. Because severe issues will not arise if one party backs down first. This year is supposed to be the year of cuteness, talkativeness, and appreciation and affection for the adults who witness it. However, you should be wary of children's squabbles. They may bring both adults into the disagreement until it becomes heated. The tale will become viral. Especially during the months that it is easy to cause discord, and frustration in married life, including the 1st Chinese month (4 Feb. - 4 Mar.), the 4th Chinese month (5 May - 4 Jun.), the 9th Chinese month (8 Oct. – 6 Nov.) and 10th Chinese month (7 Nov. – 5 Dec.).

Health

This year, the destined person's health will fluctuate between good and terrible in both cycles of life. To maintain your food clean and sanitary, elders should pay attention to it and regulate it. Keep an eye out for gastritis, intestinal illness, and hidden disorders that may arise and pose a concern. You should have a companion or someone accompany you when doing activities or traveling outside since dizziness might lead you to fall and get wounded. Especially during the months that you need to take extra care of your health, including the 1st Chinese month (4 Feb. - 4 Mar.), the 4th Chinese month (5 May - 4 Jun.), and the 9th Chinese month. (8 Oct. - 6 Nov.) and the 10th month of China (7 Nov. - 5 Dec.) Be more cautious of the possibility of damage and bleeding from road usage, and always keep an eye out for irregularities in the body. If you notice any strange symptoms, you should consult a doctor right away. Be cautious of water hazards for children during this season, whether they are participating in water sports or swimming in natural water sources. Traveling by water should be done with caution. This includes the risk of getting scalded by hot water.

Year of the MONKEY (Fire) | (1968)

" The Monkey Love in the Freedom " is a person born in the year of the MONKEY at the age of 56 years (1968)

Overview

This life cycle suggests that for the person born in the Year of the Monkey, this year will be half good and half negative. On the plus side, this year provides another opportunity to grow your firm. Work and company are heading in the right path. You may increase your effort and investment, or you can start enhancing your business to meet your objectives. Both can combine (or take over) enterprises. May you have the fortitude to invest in or acquire stocks with a future as the foundation for company development. Because investment will improve your professional growth and allow you to advance to a higher degree of prestige. In addition, auspicious and patronizing power appears to be visiting the residence. You are likely to enjoy an auspicious occasion or acquire valuable property throughout the year. A house with land or a car, and there will be opportunities throughout the year to welcome new members into the house or relocate to a new dwelling or office, a new factory, or a new house. This is another fortunate year for you. However, one must be cautious since malevolent stars, such as the wicked star Suai Pua and the star Go Xing, visit the residence throughout the year. This sometimes necessitates being wary of kids or those with evil purposes who may discreetly attack, injure, and cause problems, as well as being wary of criminals. There will be problems in the management line or arguments with coworkers on the job. Causing everyone to remain cautious rather than collaborating to achieve goals. You must also be mindful of your family members' health and safety concerns. Be cautious of mishaps that may occur on your hands or legs, or you may likely have greater discomfort this year.

Career and Business

This year, your work will lead to success. Your task will be completed. The company's growth and success will continue. As a result, it is appropriate for constructing a portfolio, developing a business, establishing branches, purchasing enterprises, or investing in other sorts of businesses. Investing will bring you unexpected profits. Especially during the months when work and investment have a bright and prosperous direction, namely the 2nd Chinese month (5 Mar. - 3 Apr.), the 3rd Chinese month (4 Apr. - 4 May), the 7th Chinese month (7 Aug. - 6 Sep.) and 11th Chinese month (6 Dec. 2024 - 4 Jan. 2025). During this year, there will be some months when business and business will take place. More chaotic problems include the 1st Chinese month (4 Feb. - 4 Mar.), the 4th Chinese month (5 May - 4 June), the 9th Chinese month (8 Oct. - 6 Nov.) and the 10th Chinese month (7 Nov. - 5 Dec.) During this time, be wary of con artists who may try to con you out of your money. When signing a purchase or sale contract, be wary of revealing clauses that conceal exploitative circumstances. As a result, you should pay close attention to the details. There will be no issues afterward.

25

Financial

Your financial fortunes will be highly erratic this year, so be wary of unforeseen capital outflows or huge, unexpected current costs that may produce a shortage of liquidity. You should avoid investing in high-risk firms or those that are likely to breach the law. Because if you're caught, you might face a hefty fine. Especially during the months when finances are in decline. You must closely manage your money in the circulating system, including the 1st Chinese month (4 Feb. - 4 Mar.), the 4th Chinese month (5 May - 4 Jun), the 9th Chinese month (8 Oct. – 6 Nov.), and the 10th Chinese month (7 Nov. – 5 Dec.) You must exercise caution when releasing accounts receivable without following up. Because problematic debts may be discovered during the year, you should expedite debt or restrict the account balance. Do not lend to anyone or sign any financial guarantees. For the months when your finances return to flowing smoothly, they are: 2nd Chinese month (5 Mar. - 3 Apr.), 3rd Chinese month (4 Apr. - 4 May), 7th Chinese month (7

Aug. - 6 Sep.), and the 11th Chinese month (6 Dec. 2024 - 4 Jan. 2025)

Family
This year's family was rough. You should pay more attention to the safety and health of the individuals in your house, especially the elderly. Be wary of odd and unexpected calamities. Be wary of people in the house getting into fights with neighbors, since this might ruin the excellent connection between the two households. You should also be wary of domestic disputes. You should also be careful of conflicts among people in the house. During the months when conflicts and chaos occur within the family, they include the 1st Chinese month (4 Feb. - 4 Mar.), the 4th Chinese month (5 May - 4 June), and the 9th month. China (8 Oct. - 6 Nov.) and the 10th month of China (7 Nov. - 5 Dec.) must be more attentive to accidents among members of the home. Be wary of small subordinates who cause problems. Keep an eye out for valuables that have been damaged, misplaced, or stolen. If you have the opportunity to conduct auspicious gatherings

within your home this year. Positive energy can assist in eliminating negative energy in the home.

Love

This year's love is a reasonable criterion. However, when you are trapped and have troubles, loving ones will assist you. In many cases, however, you must reveal the truth to people close to you. Because you communicate with each other and generate misunderstandings, the distrust will fade. Especially during the months when love and relationships are quite fragile and can easily cause quarrels with each other, including the 1st Chinese month (4 Feb. - 4 Mar.), the 4th Chinese month (5 May - 4 Jun), the 9th Chinese month (8 Oct. - 6 Nov.) and 10th Chinese month (7 Nov. - 5 Dec.) You should not interfere as a third party in other people's family connections, and you should avoid going to nightlife entertainment places since it will harm your family.

Health

This year, your physical health has suffered. Be wary of stress or overwork that might lead to sleeplessness. Inadequate rest causes the body to weaken, resulting in allergies and an increased susceptibility to infectious illnesses. However, you should practice good eating habits and select meals that are good for your health. Especially during the following months, you must be especially mindful of your health: 1st Chinese month (4 Feb. - 4 Mar.), the 4th Chinese month (5 May - 4 Jun), the 9th Chinese month (8 Oct. - 6 Nov.) and the 10th Chinese month (7 Nov. - 5 Dec.). Be careful of the recurrence of congenital diseases. diabetes, heart disease Hepatitis, food poisoning, and injuries to the hands or legs from accidents.

Year of the MONKEY (Earth) | (1980)

" The Monkey is smart" is a person born in the year of the MONKEY at the age of 44 years (1980)

Overview

This year is regarded as another fortunate year for the Year of the Monkey slated for this age cycle, in which the destined home will be on the path of wealth, renown, status, money, and honor all at the same time. You will have the option of starting a business or purchasing pricey assets to help your firm grow. It is a good time to move into a new home or apartment. Both have the prerequisites for investing in new profitable firms. However, you will experience problems this year in your home of destiny due to the unlucky force of the "Gowsing Star," which emits harmful radiation to hinder you. Your employment tasks, including your business, may frequently confront difficulties. Furthermore, it frequently causes the house owner's mood to vary, and the mind is quickly agitated. Careless speech can harm others through words said without malice. However, without recognizing it, this resulted in the creation of adversaries. Furthermore, you should not engage or interfere in the affairs of others that are not your concern. Furthermore, another malicious star arrives during the year to disrupt the house of destiny. "Star Pua Pai" will have an impact on the loss of riches and gold. As a result, you should keep a tight eye on your income and expenditure accounts. If there is a leak, it should be repaired as soon as possible. Don't let it become a major leak. Be cautious of accounts receivable that are difficult to locate and collect, resulting in bad debt accounts. Because it will generate a liquidity crisis. You should also keep an eye out for accidents when at work and traveling.

Career and Business

The work horoscope for this year has found a prosperous route. Work will advance, and business will grow. For people who are already in business and want to expand. Start or acquire a firm, form a joint venture, or participate in the stock market. Those who worked this year are eligible for a promotion and wage rise. This year, many times support and promote both your career and business to advance, including the 2nd Chinese month (5 Mar. - 3 Apr.), the 3rd Chinese month (4 Apr. - 4 May)), the 7th Chinese month (7 Aug. - 6 Sep.) and 11th Chinese month (6 Dec. 2024 - 4 Jan. 2025) for the month that you Should avoid investing and business, there are often obstacles and problems, including the 1st Chinese month (4 Feb. - 4 Mar.), the 4th Chinese month (5 May - 4 June), the 9th Chinese month (8 Oct. - 6 Nov.) and the 10th Chinese month (7 Nov. - 5 Dec.) Investing should be avoided during this time. Because foreign economic movements will be impacted. Insiders or partners may also be corrupt. Furthermore, you should be wary of fraudsters who try to con you out of your money. When signing an employment contract or being employed for work, make sure there are no minor provisions in the contract. It will become an issue later.

Financial

This year is the year of bountiful income. Cash inflows, whether direct from salaries or sales of goods and services, are expected to increase. Money obtained as a result of special employment, such as bonuses, commissions, dividends, money from the Government Savings Bank label, or money from fortune. There will be an option to receive more funds. This includes people who are considering starting their firm. You will be able to establish a store or purchase your own business this year. May you find the strength to continue forward and grab the opportunity to realize your aspirations. Especially the months in which your finances are flowing smoothly, including 2nd Chinese month (5 Mar. - 3 Apr.), the 3rd Chinese month (4 Apr. - 4 May), the 7th Chinese month (7 Aug. - 6 Sep.), and the 11th Chinese month (6 Dec. 2024 - 4 Jan. 2025). However, you should be careful during the months when your finances will be tight and there will be unexpected expenses, including 1st Chinese month (4 Feb. – 4 Mar.), the 4th Chinese month (5 May – 4 Jun), 9th Chinese month (8 Oct. – 6 Nov.), and 10th Chinese month. (7 Nov. - 5 Dec.) Be careful of financial leakage points. You should refrain from gambling. Do not lend money or sign financial guarantees and do not invest or engage in illegal business.

Family

The family horoscope for this year is smooth. The power of riches and favorable patronage pays a visit. There will be a chance to purchase pricey real estate. It might be the acquisition of a home with land, an automobile, or a commercial enterprise. There is a good moment to move into a new home. There will also be good occurrences in the house. Adult birthday parties can be held in the house. This year, radiant fortunate energy will flow throughout the house, creating smiles and enjoyment. But you cannot be careless about the following months where chaotic events will occur, namely the 1st Chinese month (4 Feb. - 4 Mar.), the 4th Chinese month (5 May - 4 Jun.), the 9th Chinese month (8 Oct. - 6 Nov.) and the 10th Chinese month (7 Nov. - 5 Dec.). You should avoid arguing with your family or fighting with your neighbors. Be wary of threats from kids or subordinates who intend to stir problems. Such as damaging or losing things or having a robber break into the residence.

Love

This year will be half nice and three parts horrible in terms of love. You should, however, make more time for your loved one's family than you do. Don't claim to be busy as an excuse. It is a conscious decision to leave love alone and distant. Because this will lead to further conflicts and worsen the fissures. Furthermore, the malevolent star Gou Sing will affect you at the base of love, causing you to be easily upset with your sweetheart. Be wary of turning away to find transient love elsewhere. It will add additional gasoline to the flames of domestic strife. Especially during the months when love problems can easily occur, including the 1st Chinese month (4 Feb. - 4 Mar.), the 4th Chinese month (5 May - 4 Jun), the 9th Chinese month (8 Oct. - 6 Nov.), and the 10th Chinese month (7 Nov. - 5 Dec.) Be careful of quarrels from irrational behavior that goes astray to the point of causing love to break up.

Health

This year's health horoscope is favorable. Stress problems that induce insomnia or inadequate sleep should be avoided. It will degrade the body's health and make it feeble. You should pay special attention to your nutrition. Choose sanitary foods. Avoid excessive consumption of alcohol and other intoxicants, including smoking. Keep an eye out for gastritis and inflammatory bowel illness. Especially during the months that you need to take extra care and attention to your health, including the 1st Chinese month (4 Feb. - 4 Mar.), the 4th Chinese month (5 May - 4 Jun), the 9th Chinese month (8 Oct. - 6 Nov.) and 10th Chinese month (7 Nov. - 5 Dec.) Keep an eye out for workplace accidents. Take precautions to avoid injury when driving. Especially if you're attending a party. After consuming alcohol You should not operate a motor vehicle. To be safe, you should take public transit first.

Year of the MONKEY (Water) | (1992)

" The monkey is climbing a tree." is a person born in the year of the MONKEY at the age of 32 years (1992)

Overview

This year, the Year of the Monkey, which will be 32 years old, is another favorable moment to face the power of patronage. Both are empowered and supported by the fortunate stars that shine brilliantly. When fortunate energy arrives to aid and encourage you, you will come across rare possibilities. So don't let time get away from you. This year will provide an opportunity to make a positive difference. As a result, whether you plan or hope for something, you must proceed with a purpose and not be sidetracked by the cacophony of opposition. However, you must improve your diligence and develop yourself to stay up with the changing situations around you. Dare to take on a large task and go forward to capture an opportunity. You will be able to start your own business or expand your current one to accommodate the future sales increase. This year's financial fortunes will be thick and bountiful. This year, fame, position, social standing, and fortune will all come together. However, you must not overlook the risks of the malevolent star Xiao Ying, who frequently has an impact on your subordinates or servants, producing issues, headaches, or property loss. Furthermore, disagreements between employees in the firm must be avoided. Take caution not to let disagreements stymie your job advancement. To fix the situation, you must be aware and apply compromise when mediating. Don't become emotional or resort to violence to solve problems. Because it will exacerbate the situation and stymie future improvement.

Career and Business

This year will be prosperous, and work will progress. The company may grow and sell well. May you find the strength to reconsider and act again. Replace the old and outmoded regulatory system with modern technologies. The environment will appear brighter. Today's vigilance lays the groundwork for a secure tomorrow. Especially if you strike when the iron is hot during the months that support and promote you, namely the 2nd Chinese month (5 Mar. - 3 Apr.), the 3rd Chinese month (4 Apr. - 4 May).) 7 Chinese month (7 Aug. - 6 Sep.) and the 11th Chinese month (6 Dec. 2024 - 4 Jan. 2025) In addition, new job opportunities, cooperative partnerships, and diverse investments. Overall, improvement will be made this year. As a result, we urge that you select to invest in a firm with a future with the proper personnel. It will be a criterion for receiving a gratifying dividend return when combined with the preparedness of your funds. As for the months when work and trade will encounter problems and obstacles, they include the 1st Chinese month (4 Feb. - 4 Mar.), the 4th Chinese month (5 May - 4 June), the 9th Chinese month (8 Oct. - 6 Nov.) and the 10th Chinese month (7 Nov. - 5 Dec.) Work may result in mistakes at this time. As a result, evaluating the job in person will assist in avoiding mistakes or unanticipated market changes that may cause harm to the work. When signing job contracts or accepting employment, use caution. Always consider deliberately and thoroughly before acting. You will bring yourself problems if you are attentive to others.

Financial

This year has been a financial success. Money will come in from a variety of sources depending on how much you have invested. However, this year, I want you to be more diligent and to strive to the fullest. The more diligent you are, the more riches you will receive. Especially during the months when your finances have good liquidity, namely the 2nd Chinese month (5 Mar. - 3 Apr.), the 3rd Chinese month (4 Apr. - 4 May), the 7th Chinese month (7 Aug. - 6 Sep.) and the 11th Chinese month (6 Dec. 2024 - 4 Jan. 2025). However, you should be careful during the following months when finances will encounter a lack of liquidity and unexpected expenses including 1st Chinese month (4 Feb. - 4 Mar.), 4th Chinese month (5 May - 4 Jun), the 9th Chinese month (8 Oct. - 6 Nov.) and the 10th Chinese month (7 Nov. - 5 Dec.) prohibit others from lending money or signing financial guarantees. Do not be greedy, do not gamble, do not do business that is against the laws of the country.

Family

This year, families will encounter the power of patronage. It is possible that you may receive excellent news or that lucky circumstances will occur. You will be able to purchase pricey real estate. There is an auspicious time to move into a new house or residence, or new members of the house may be added, or members of the house may become famous and respectable in some way. As a result, others who witness it will see it as respectable and admirable. But you should be careful during the months when problems and chaos will arise in your family, including the 1st Chinese month (4 Feb. - 4 Mar.), the 4th Chinese month (5 May - 4 Jun), the 9th Chinese month (8 Oct. - 6 Nov.) and 10th Chinese month (7 Nov. - 5 Dec.) where you must be aware of home safety and should take care of the elderly in the house attentively. Be wary of accidents or unforeseen incidents that may result in property damage. Problems with conflicts, whether within the house or with neighbors, should be avoided, as should valuables being destroyed, lost, or stolen. Furthermore, you should avoid becoming involved in disputes among friends. You should be cautious when establishing new pals. You may be duped or taken advantage of.

Love

The love horoscope for this year is very easy. This year will bring a tantrum for those who are intended to be single, causing them to meet their true match but end up marrying. You must return to examine the conditions of the good fortune that you have created together. Those who already have a spouse or partner should always preserve their love for it to grow properly. But don't be careless and let the bad star lead you astray. Your marriage will undoubtedly fail. The months during which you should support your love so that arguments and problems do not occur include the 1st Chinese month (4 Feb. - 4 Mar.), the 4th Chinese month (5 May - 4 Jun), the 9th Chinese month (8 Oct. - 6 Nov.) and 10th Chinese month (7 Nov. - 5 Dec.) must be more cautious. Control your actions more tightly. You should also avoid visiting entertainment places since they might cause love to end and families to be ripped apart.

Health

For your health this year overall is good. If there is only a slight illness, it can be easily treated. But if you enter the following months, you must turn to increasing care and attention to your health, including the 1st Chinese month (4 Feb. - 4 Mar.), the 4th Chinese month (5 May - 4 Jun.), the 9th Chinese month (8 Oct. - 6 Nov.) and 10th Chinese month (7 Nov. - 5 Dec.) You should avoid driving a car if you attend a party or visit a society where drinking and partying with alcohol and intoxicants is unavoidable. Also, when posing, make sure no one else is in the frame. It will irritate you to the point of danger and may cause injury. You must be cautious, especially when it comes to individuals who organize calls or protests.

Chinese Astrology Horoscope for Each Month

Month 12 in the Rabbit Year (6 Jan 23 - 3 Feb 23)
This month marks the start of the new year. Because the Year of the Monkey is having another prosperous year. To bring the lucky moment to win at the start of the year. Plan objectives for the entire year to support them so that you have a direction rather than drifting aimlessly. By evaluating lessons learned from prior mistakes to determine what needs to be changed and fixed, then fill in for the better. This month is another ideal time for persons born in the Year of the Monkey to grow. To have a solid direction and favorable outcomes, you need to carefully consider the time and possibilities that come your way and accelerate your initial sales in the first month.

This salary horoscope is sufficient. As a result, you should not expect to make money from gambling or speculating in other industries, and you should not sign financial assurances for others. Concerning work, particularly commercial enterprise, monsoon clouds are covering it throughout this season, causing unsmoothness for workers at both the top and lower levels of the company. As a result, establishing strong relationships with one another and always improving ties with those around you. It will assist you in overcoming this issue. This is not the time to engage in joint ventures or new investments in other enterprises and should be postponed for the time being.

Family horoscopes are in disarray. Keep an eye out for medical bills for the elderly in the home. To prevent criminals from taking your valuables, you should take care of them and keep them in a secure location.

If your love horoscope is favorable and the moment is favorable, you will have the option to participate in tourist tours or as a volunteer to serve society.

If your health is poor, be wary of heart disease, liver disease, and the accumulation of ailments caused by overindulgent eating. As for relatives and friends, be wary of encountering people with ill intentions who come and deceive.

Support Days: 1 Jan., 5 Jan., 9 Jan., 13 Jan., 17 Jan., 21 Jan., 25 Jan., 29 Jan.
Lucky Days: 6 Jan., 18 Jan., 30 Jan.
Misfortune Days: 3 Jan., 15 Jan., 27 Jan.
Bad Days: 12 Jan., 24 Jan.

Month 1 in the Dragon Year (4 Feb 23 - 5 Mar 23)
Those born in the Year of the Monkey this month may suffer monsoon issues because the malicious star Sapphire emerges in the house of fate, extending its power. Focusing on it will generate barriers and troubles in your career and business. Be wary of unforeseen intervening events that might result in losses. As a result, avoid investing in numerous sectors during this period. During this month, you should either work or accept the job. You must primarily assess your talents and develop two or three backup plans to deal with unforeseen circumstances.

This salary will see a mix of good and unpleasant things, but income will continue to flow unabated. However, at this time, you should be cautious of unforeseen costs that might drain your bank account. As a result, no matter what, you must stick to saving methods, cut out superfluous spending, discover ways to increase your income through other channels, and not lend money to others or engage in illicit transactions. Because you risk losing both people and money. This month, there is a chance that errors may occur at work or in business, resulting in property damage. Disturbances will arise with the folks you must negotiate with.

During this time, you should avoid establishing a new career, investing in stocks, and investing in new stuff. Be wary about getting duped by fraudsters. The family horoscope is serene. Members of the house adore and support one another. But the romantic aspect is bleak. It seems like a severe downpour is on its way. To avoid division, you should regulate your emotions and act within your boundaries. Your general health is still good but drive with extreme caution. Take no chances. In terms of family and friends, avoid interfering in your friends' relationships.

Support Days: 2 Feb., 6 Feb., 10 Feb., 14 Feb., 18 Feb., 22 Feb., 26 Feb.
Lucky Days: 11 Feb., 23 Feb.
Misfortune Days: 8 Feb., 20 Feb.
Bad Days: 5 Feb., 17 Feb., 29 Feb.

Month 2 in the Dragon Year (6 Mar 23 - 5 Apr 23)
With the arrival of this month, the Year of the Monkey person's life path shifts towards the alliance line. The fortunate star "Kok Ying" is also circling to encourage and assist. It's like the sky after a rainstorm, where the rainbow shines brightly. Various occurrences begin to calm down, and your work becomes more fluid. The company will do well and generate a profit. It is another period when fortunate energy visits and it is a terrific chance that comes only once a year. What you should do during this period is work or invest in something you've

been thinking about. May this month go as easily as possible and as quickly as possible. If the funds, staff, and plans are in place. Move quickly, don't waste time, and don't let a good chance pass you by.

This pay increase is a source of abundance. Cash inflows come in two forms. Hands are used to accept money via gambling, speculation, or windfalls. However, you should not be greedy and overinvest. It will not be worthwhile. The main thing is that you work with endurance, dedication, and determination. Work is a source of income, as is obtaining assistance from coworkers and adults. As a result, you should not wait. Turn on the green light to go as planned to your destination. Because if you only contemplate, hesitate, and wait to make a decision, you may lose out and be taken advantage of by others.

The family horoscope is tranquil. Patronage pays a visit and might plan fortunate events. They may add members or have a nice time and relocate to a different house or residence. It is the time of year when the love tree blooms and gives fruit. Both are good occasions to be married or enter the palace. Health and well-being For family and friends who have horoscopes to back them up, they suggest that dealing with challenging situations may not be as difficult as they thought. Because you'll find someone who can show you how to get out. It is possible to begin a new employment, buy stocks, and make different investments.

Support Days: 1 Mar, 5 Mar., 9 Mar., 13 Mar., 17 Mar., 21 Mar., 25 Mar., 29 Mar.
Lucky Days: 6 Mar, 18 Mar., 30 Mar.
Misfortune Days: 3 Mar, 15 Mar., 27 Mar.
Bad Days: 12 Mar, 24 Mar.

Month 3 in the Dragon Year (6 Apr 23 - 5 May 23)
This month, the path of persons born in the Year of the Monkey enters the alliance area once more. Furthermore, fortunate stars provide assistance and encouragement to the Destiny House. Make the way light, and the power of patronage shines through, allowing you to see the path to riches. This month, you

should work on turning your former flaws and disadvantages into strengths. When the door of a good time opens, rush to seize it, daring to go forward, locate an opportunity, and dare to begin something new. Whether at work or in business, everything runs well. Negotiating is like being given the green light to lead the way. Furthermore, getting into joint ventures or investing in the stock market all enjoy patronage and encouragement. It is stated that if you simply sit and bend your hands and feet, you will be able to. Don't rush to grasp this fantastic opportunity and transform your labor into money that will grow. You could sit and cry for a long time.

In terms of labor and business, as well as having a progressive and lucrative path. There is still the ability to encourage investment and grow things further. You can purchase outside firms, break lines, open new branches, or expand on existing ones. You will receive a monetary return in a lovely account. The money is ample for this wage. Cash will enter the system in a variety of ways. Furthermore, there is a potential of winning a huge sum of money through gambling. But just don't go overboard and spend it all. Because the money will not be returned in the end.

The family side is tranquil. Relatives and friends are all supportive and helpful. This month you will make genuine pals. This will assist in identifying new strategies to grow money.

The love horoscope is favorable. People who love freely are both useful and a safe place to confide in one's sorrow. For those of you who are still single and haven't found love. If you are comfortable sharing your life with someone, this is the month to express your feelings. Because your good hands will grasp it first if you're sluggish. If you are in good health, even if you become ill, you will have a good doctor to assist you in treating your ailment.

Support Days: 2 Apr., 6 Apr., 10 Apr., 14 Apr., 18 Apr., 22 Apr., 26 Apr., 30 Apr
Lucky Days: 11 Apr., 23 Apr.

Misfortune Days: 8 Apr., 20 Apr.
Bad Days: 5 Apr., 17 Apr., 29 Apr.

Month 4 in the Dragon Year (6 May 23 - 5 Jun 23)
This month, the house of fate of people born in the Year of the Monkey has moved to face the opposing forces. The malevolent constellations Go Xing and Gao Ka also seemed to control and torment. Our destiny's course has shifted to zero. As a result, every task should be performed with more caution. The rainfall had an impact on work and business. There will be disagreements inside the agency. Minor subordinates cause issues, and there will be external disruptions. Those who form alliances at this time should be wary of corruption. Be wary of being duped while creating long-term binding contract paperwork. This month, you should exercise self-control and refrain from breaking ranks or deviating from your responsibilities. Do your job well. Keep an eye out for strikes or rioting inside the organization. You should also be cautious about reacting to folks who irritate you with your emotions. Fighting back with force will be like

putting gasoline on a fire, causing more violence to erupt. Starting jobs, buying stocks, and investing during this time are all bad ideas.

This salary fate is not favorable. You might lose a substantial chunk of money unexpectedly. As a result, do not incur any new commitments or debts. By gambling, trying your luck, or assessing your luck in various stock lottery games. Also, avoid high-risk or unlawful activities. Make no loans or financial commitments. Be wary about being duped into losing money. The family situation is bad. Avoid having disagreements with your neighbors. Take a deep breath and a step back. Don't be impatient and start making plans. You will be protected, but be aware that unexpected things may occur to members of the household.

In terms of health, watch out for gastritis, intestinal sickness, and digestive system inflammation. You should avoid meals containing fire elements, particularly foods that are hot when consumed.

Love, on the other hand, suffices. Just don't be arrogant or self-centered, and avoid traveling to places of fun to avoid becoming infected with deadly illnesses.

In terms of family and friends, one should avoid people who frequently lure one into vices.

Support Days: 4 May., 8 May., 12 May., 16 May., 20 May., 24 May., 28 May.
Lucky Days: 5 May., 17 May., 29 May.
Misfortune Days: 2 May., 14 May., 26 May.
Bad Days: 11 May., 23 May.

Month 5 in the Dragon Year (6 Jun 23 - 6 Jul 23)
The horoscope is still in a downward spiral as we begin this month. Because the house of destiny shifts and collides with an evil star. As a result, when engaging in various activities, you must remain cool and avoid displaying emotions. The greater the impact force, the harder it is. In terms of employment, be prepared to encounter individuals with evil intentions who are constantly seeking difficulties, and be prepared to deal with

intricate issues that are waiting for you to hurry about and repair them. As a result, you should carefully consider your work before committing to it. The monsoon intervened, preventing the commercial venture from proceeding as planned. What you should do this month is determine whether or not to stick to your plan. Please make every effort to continue. Do not listen to other people's voices to distract your thoughts. Even if you experience certain difficulties, please battle with effort and patience. The issues will be fixed on their own.

Even when there are monsoons, the issue in work and business may be rectified due to the actual dedication and diligence of the chosen individual. They all give support and assistance in resolving various challenges, including families and friends. This month, you must be gentle and strong to support your task properly. This pay is a volatile measure of fortune. Be wary of unexpected costs that drain your bank account and cause it to become insolvent. As a result, you should refrain from gambling. Invest in transactions that are likely to break the law, such as piracy. Because you will be penalized and may face legal action as a consequence.

The riches of the family have found tranquility. When it comes to love, be cautious while making commitments. It has to be real and true, or else you won't be able to accomplish it. Don't simply say it to make the other person feel awful for no reason.

This month's health horoscope does not reveal any signs of major sickness that should concern you.

Consider your readiness while starting a new career, investing in stocks, or making other investments. Whether it is a matter of money, time spent working together, or even the partner's credentials. If you are not yet ready, postponing is the best option.

Support Days: 1 Jun., 5 Jun., 9 Jun., 13 Jun., 17 Jun., 21 Jun., 25 Jun., 29 Jun.
Lucky Days: 10 Jun., 22 Jun.
Misfortune Days: 7 Jun., 19 Jun.

Bad Days: 4 Jun., 16 Jun., 28 Jun.

Month 6 in the Dragon Year (7 Jul 23 - 7 Aug 23)
This month, the Year of the Monkey's Destiny has shifted to the penalty area. As a result, the life graph varies and is not stable. It's as if the battery is weak and there isn't enough power to fly, leading the fortunes to tumble. During this time, occurrences of blocking and obstruction are common, forcing individuals to crash head-on and back, and many good possibilities are lost. This month, you should examine your available strength and make the most of it. During this time, decisions must be made with greater caution, but they must also be definitive. Otherwise, the water may fail and the consequences will be minor.

You will face obstacles, issues, and pressures both inside and outside your line of employment. Relationships will have trouble breaking down boundaries if they are not very solid during this phase. As a result, you should cultivate positive interpersonal relationships with those around you and be respectful to adults. Furthermore, be extra cautious with any contract paperwork that will be handled during this period to avoid being duped and put at a disadvantage. Do not be impatient or act according to your wishes when performing various activities throughout this period. Be open to hearing other coworkers' perspectives as well.

The income in this pay horoscope is moderate. Gambling should be prohibited. You should not want riches that are not yours. You should budget cautiously. Anything that isn't required should be eliminated first. This includes forbidding lending money or signing any form of financial promise.

Peace is excellent for the family fortune. You will, however, encounter family and friends that invite you to lose.

The fate of love is fragile; be careful not to be soft-hearted; keep your heart firmly in mind; don't just be affected by someone and your heart will be swayed and diverted.

In terms of health, you should still be cautious about the possibility of bleeding from an accident. This includes being cautious about hand, leg, or facial injuries.

In terms of beginning a new career, investing in stocks, and making other decisions. This month, you should avoid all types of investments.

Support Days: 3 Jul., 7 Jul., 11 Jul., 15 Jul., 19 Jul., 23 Jul., 27 Jul., 31 Jul.
Lucky Days: 4 Jul., 16 Jul., 28 Jul.
Misfortune Days: 1 Jul., 13 Jul., 25 Jul.
Bad Days: 10 Jul., 22 Jul.

Month 7 in the Dragon Year (8 Aug 23 - 7 Sep 23)
This month, the Year of the Monkey's life path has progressed beyond the influence of bad influences. Meet the brilliantly sparkling auspicious stars, resulting in a smooth and dazzling surface. It will be a moment of good fortune and pleasant sailing for you. Work and the company will undergo positive transformations. During this time, you should

continue to build on what is still unresolved. Prepare investment factors based on your objectives. Furthermore, you should be open to listening to the ideas of others around you to gain knowledge for your advantage and work hard consistently to advance to the next level.

This is a good starting pay. Even though you continue to earn money. However, the action may result in significant capital outflows. As a result, the action of raising mats should be halted. Reduced entertainment will assist in balancing income and spending without generating a lack of cash. Work, even commercial enterprise, is still the path of least resistance. As a result, you must work hard to develop work to meet the sales objective. This includes hastening the drive for certain initiatives. Because it is a terrific moment for a variety of reasons. Furthermore, you should cultivate positive relationships with individuals around you or with those with whom you must interact, especially consumers. To build ties and establish groups to rely on one another in times of crisis.

According to the family's horoscope, favorable energy is visiting. An auspicious event may be taking place within the house, or it may be an auspicious moment to move into a new house or residence. Love horoscope is a time to earn points; you can buy the correct stuff to wow your spouse and sweetheart. However, in terms of health, be cautious of sudden bleeding, as well as infectious disorders and allergies. Starting a new career, buying stocks, and making other investments are all options. You should still use caution when investing money since you may experience more losses than rewards.

Support Days: 4 Aug., 8 Aug., 12 Aug., 16 Aug., 20 Aug., 24 Aug., 28 Aug.
Lucky Days: 9 Aug., 21 Aug.
Misfortune Days: 6 Aug., 18 Aug., 30 Aug.
Bad Days: 3 Aug., 15 Aug., 27 Aug..

Month 8 in the Dragon Year (8 Sep 23 - 7 Oct 23)
Those born in the Year of the Monkey will have a 50/50 chance of good and bad luck. This is because wicked stars will arrive in this month

to concentrate and torment. At the same time, fortunate stars are circling in to shine together. What you should do at this time is keep your job and duties hidden and establish a firm foundation. Don't be impatient or irresponsible in what you think, read, or do. Every endeavor needs perseverance and foresight. Furthermore, any legal contracts made at this time must be cautious.

During this time in your job and business, there will be disagreements in your field of work. Be wary of becoming provoked by individuals who do not want you well, since this may lead to disaster. As a result, please do your best to fulfill your tasks and responsibilities. Interfering with each other's job will aid in the reduction of issues and harassment. This compensation is quite variable. Even if there is revenue, there will be costs that will balance each other out. As a result, taking risks in gambling and speculating is still not advised. Make no loans or financial commitments. Attempt to maintain a perfect balance between income and spending. Do not take any unnecessary risks with your money.

In this family horoscope, be wary of illness in the family, as well as kids or slaves making problems in neighboring households. There is nothing to be concerned about in terms of love and relationships. What single individuals are waiting for will bring them success. If you sincerely love each other and want to marry, you should stay near to win one other's heart. However, the health of grilled and fried foods is not excellent since the heat causes numerous ailments to follow.

Relatives and friends are weary of statements that are not meant to offend those who listen. Starting a new career, investing in stocks, and making other investments all require careful consideration. Don't take a tiny salary for granted because it may deplete your savings later.

Support Days: 1 Sep, 5 Sep., 9 Sep, 13 Sep, 17 Sep., 21 Sep., 25 Sep., 29 Sep.

Lucky Days: 2 Sep, 14 Sep., 26 Sep.
Misfortune Days: 11 Sep, 23 Sep.
Bad Days: 8 Sep, 20 Sep.

Month 9 in the Dragon Year (8 Oct 23 - 6 Nov 23)
This month, your fortune has once again crossed the line of danger. Thus emerged the power of impediment. The life path is fraught with peril. The path of fate is winding and rocky. Many things you want and aim to be careful about will turn out to be unexpected or shift into an entirely surprising narrative. Work will present challenges, as will business and competition. You must be cautious since significant consumers tend to defect and switch to competition. This month, you should engage in a variety of work tasks. During this time, do not be impatient or careless. You should also be truthful in your work, particularly when faults are discovered. You must be willing to accept responsibility for the task you are in charge of.

This salary horoscope is not favorable. There is a property loss threshold. Income is low, and costs are lurking in the shadows. You may also face unforeseen bills that strain your finances. Internal disputes and instability must still be avoided in company and commerce. As a result, one should refrain from interfering with the work of others. You should also be objective when solving difficulties. You must make a firm decision. But don't get too worked up over it since it will just make things worse. When signing any business contract, you must pay close attention to the details, avoid being misled to your disadvantage, and be wary of cheaters who come to deceive and swindle you.

The family horoscope is not favorable. Keep an eye out for house accidents and robbers breaking in. The love horoscope for this month faces monsoon waves. Relationships are delicate, therefore avoid events that can cause conflict. You should also avoid interfering in other people's family ties as a third party. To avoid getting sick, avoid wandering about in entertainment places.

In terms of health, you should continue to focus on clean drinking and eating habits. Be cautious of hazards when drinking alcohol and driving on the road. This month, don't trust family or friends; expose everything, and be cautious; trouble will follow.

When starting a new career, investing in stocks, or making other investments, you must still carefully evaluate environmental aspects. Don't invest money if you aren't ready.

Support Days: 3 Oct., 7 Oct., 11 Oct., 15 Oct., 19 Oct., 23 Oct., 27 Oct., 31 Oct.
Lucky Days: 8 Oct., 20 Oct.
Misfortune Days: 5 Oct., 17 Oct., 29 Oct.
Bad Days: 2 Oct., 14 Oct., 26 Oct.

Month 10 in the Dragon Year (7 Nov 23 - 6 Dec 23)

This month's destiny criterion for people born in the Year of the Monkey is still experiencing monsoons. Because of the emergence of a swarm of evil stars who upset and disturb the mansion of fate. Problems and roadblocks began to surface gradually. However, you are still fortunate in that favorable stars will shine and assist you throughout the month. Many things that appear bleak will have beneficial transformations. As a result, there are several things you should avoid doing this month, especially, doing nothing under this counter-current and unpredictable circumstance. You should keep yourself alive and wait for an appropriate opportunity to proceed with your task. However, if an issue is discovered, the level of criticality of the problem should be divided. Solve the problem from large to small points. To go forward, you should always prepare in every element, including the work system plan, and know how to position the correct personnel for the task. In terms of work, you are still in the grip of a pressure storm. You will ultimately discover a solution and have someone aid you to show you the road if you only have a determined heart and don't give up and give up halfway.

Even if there is a typical flow of revenue, this salary fortune has a middling income. However, you should first follow the rules of frugality. Furthermore, one should not be greedy and expect to get rich quickly by engaging in criminal business or gambling, or by playing the stock lottery. Remind yourself not to be greedy to avoid falling into the traps of others. The family horoscope is serene. There is greater delicacy and subtlety. There were also no misfortunes to be concerned about.

The loving side is silky. This month is a good time to propose love, reconciliation, engagement, or marriage.

If your health is in good shape, be wary of headaches and nerve pain in numerous locations produced by the body's accumulated stress and lack of proper rest.

Starting a new career, getting into stocks, and investing are all bad ideas that should be avoided for the time being.

Support Days: 4 Nov., 8 Nov., 12 Nov., 16 Nov., 20 Nov., 24 Nov., 28 Nov.

Lucky Days: 1 Nov., 13 Nov., 25 Nov.
Misfortune Days: 10 Nov., 22 Nov.
Bad Days: 7 Nov., 19 Nov.

Month 11 in the Dragon Year (7 Dec 23 - 5 Jan 24)
This month marks the end of the Year of the Monkey, however, the general trend has improved. However, the fallout from job challenges and business issues has not been handled. As a result, on this occasion, you should utilize your gained knowledge to solve blocked difficulties, try to discover the underlying cause, and completely clean it up. Allow it to pass quickly so that it does not become a weight, weighing you down and preventing your task from progressing.

This wage is consistent. The money continues to flow in two directions. As a result, the more diligent you improve yourself, the more money you will have in your pocket. You can also invest based on your objectives. Simply double-check the money in your wallet before investing to avoid roadblocks along the route.

This season is going well in terms of job and business. You should, however, be mindful of human interactions, whether with consumers, commercial partners, or authorities within the same department or company. You should maintain and improve your ties. It will result in smoother work with no monsoons getting in the way.

A good family horoscope might be helpful. There was no noise inside the home.

You've come to see the devil's star because you're in love. This allows you to fall into the charm trap and make mistakes more easily. You must exercise caution since you have the propensity to rely on emotion rather than logic. This necessitates self-control and mindfulness. A reminder to let go and be kind in minor problems, avoiding conflicts since they will cause the relationship to fall apart.

In terms of health this month, be wary of high blood pressure and the hazards of consuming too much booze. Seasonal epidemics should also be avoided.

Starting a new job can be accomplished by purchasing stocks and making other investments.

Support Days: 2 Dec., 6 Dec., 10 Dec., 14 Dec., 18 Dec., 22 Dec., 26 Dec., 30 Dec.
Lucky Days: 7 Dec., 19 Dec., 31 Dec.
Misfortune Days: 4 Dec., 16 Dec., 28 Dec.
Bad Days: 1 Dec., 13 Dec., 25 Dec.

Amulet for The Year of the Monkey

"God of Chai Sing of the South: The god of calling for wealth."

This year, those born in the Year of the Monkey should set up and worship sacred things. Place the "God of Chai Sing of the South" (god of attracting money) on your work or cash desk to improve your fortune. To request His Majesty's permission to promote and expand auspicious things for them to appear. There will be advancement and prosperity, as well as fortune and boundless wealth. A happy and calm family only provides good fortune to the owner of destiny.

A chapter in the Department of Advanced Feng Shui discusses the gods who will come to reside in the mia keng (house of fate) for the year. They are gods capable of bringing both good and terrible fortune to the god of fate in that year. When this is the case, worship will improve your luck with the gods that visit you on your birthday. As a consequence, it is said to produce positive benefits and have the most impact on you. To relied on god's power to protect him when his fortunes declined and his miseries were lessened. At the same time, you are asking for his blessings to help your business run smoothly and to provide you and your family success and prosperity.

Beware of being slandered and blamed, generating aggravation and bewilderment, if you were born in the year of the Monkey or Mia Keng (house of fate). As a result, you will have many disagreements with people and will have challenges as a result of huge spending that exceeds your expectations. If you're thinking of taking a speculative risk, get rid of any greedy ideas. If you don't want to lose money, be wary of people who will deceive you.

In terms of health, you should take extra precautions to avoid chronic illness. While the woman is in love, the male may feel abandoned. The lady will have a strong possibility of falling in love and marrying. If you want to solve an issue, you should surround yourself with sacred things and wear auspicious pendants. "God Chai Sing of the South" (god of calling for money) to request his strength and prestige to aid in the flow of wealth and gold in plenty, as well as the creation of peace and happiness in labor and commercial growth.

"Wu Lu Chaishen" or "Five Gods of Fortune" is a good fortune deity who lives in five directions: north, south, center, west, and east. They are frequently seen in Chinese shrines and temples. The fifth day of Chinese New Year (Qiu Hong) is traditionally celebrated as the birthday of the five gods, and it is a popular day for worship and blessings. "The God of Wu Lu Chaishen" is a good fortune deity who promotes livelihood and commerce at the start of the new year. In all five places in the home, light incense and beg for blessings. It is expected to help grow the business. Experiencing riches and wealth, success and prosperity will come no matter which direction you turn. Every day, money becomes wealthier, richer in every direction because the five gods are present in every area.

The god Caixing of the south, whose name is "God Cao Zhi Zhe," which is the deity of summoning money and precious goods to give to people who own them to worship, enhances the fortunes of individuals born in the Year of the Monkey this year. Those who worship Chai Xing (God of calling for prosperity) "God of Chao Chai Si Je" will assist you in avoiding and escaping calamities and perils. It also aids in increasing business and riches, as well as dissolving different bad luck and calamities, making life a total bliss experience, replete with prosperity and all dreams realized.

Those born in the Year of the Monkey should also wear an auspicious pendant. Wear "God of Chai Sing of the South" (God of calling for prosperity) around your neck or take it with you when traveling both close and far. Prosperity and advancement in business and employment are required for the owner of his destiny to be filled with money and a favorable position. All year, the family is tranquil and joyful. It generates greater and faster efficiency and effectiveness than previously.

Good Direction: Northwest, Southeast, and Southwest
Bad Direction: Northeast
Lucky Colors: White, Yellow, Gold, and Blue.
Lucky Times: 9.00 – 10.59, 15.00 – 16.59, 23.00 – 00.59.
Bad Times: 03.00 – 04.59, 21.00 – 22.59.

Good Luck For 2024

Printed in Great Britain
by Amazon